Beyoncé

Boundary-Breaking Singer & Entrepreneur

by Grace Hansen

Abdo
LEADING BIOGRAPHIES
Kids

Abdo Kids Jumbo is an Imprint of Abdo Kids
abdobooks.com

abdobooks.com

Published by Abdo Kids, a division of ABDO, P.O. Box 398166, Minneapolis, Minnesota 55439.

Printed in the United States of America, North Mankato, Minnesota.

052024

092024

THIS BOOK CONTAINS RECYCLED MATERIALS

Photo Credits: Alamy, AP Images, Getty Images, Shutterstock

Production Contributors: Teddy Borth, Jennie Forsberg, Grace Hansen
Design Contributors: Candice Keimig, Pakou Moua

Library of Congress Control Number: 2023948663

Publisher's Cataloging-in-Publication Data

Names: Hansen, Grace, author.

Title: Beyoncé: boundary-breaking singer & entrepreneur / by Grace Hansen

Other title: boundary-breaking singer & entrepreneur

Description: Minneapolis, Minnesota : Abdo Kids, 2025 | Series: Leading biographies | Includes online resources and index.

Identifiers: ISBN 9798384900733 (lib. bdg.) | ISBN 9798384901433 (ebook) | ISBN 9798384901785 (Read-to-me eBook)

Subjects: LCSH: Knowles, Beyoncé, 1981---Juvenile literature. | Women singers--United States--Biography--Juvenile literature. | Rhythm and blues musicians--Biography--Juvenile literature. | Businesswomen--Biography--Juvenile literature. | Popular music--Juvenile literature. | Actors & actresses--Biography--Juvenile literature.

Classification: DDC 782.42163--dc23

Table of Contents

Beyoncé's Beginnings

Beyoncé Giselle Knowles was born September 4, 1981. She grew up in Houston, Texas, with her parents and younger sister Solange.

Houston
Texas

Beyoncé was a natural performer from a young age. Her interests in dancing and singing began in elementary school. At just 7 years old, she won her school's talent show.

Beyoncé
Solange

Destiny's Child

When Beyoncé was 9, she joined a hip-hop group called Girls Tyme. The group changed its name to Destiny's Child in 1997. Destiny's Child became one of the best-selling girl groups of all time.

Destiny's Child
Beyoncé
Girls Tyme

Going Solo

Beyoncé also wanted to create her own music. Her first solo album, *Dangerously in Love*, **debuted** in 2003. In 2005, Destiny's Child decided to part ways.

Beyoncé released three more albums in 2006, 2008, and 2011. By this time, she was one of the biggest celebrities in the world!

In 2013, Beyoncé sang at President Barack Obama's **inauguration**. This was a special **honor**. Later that year, she released her self-titled album *Beyoncé*.

Beyoncé broke records with her sixth studio album, *Lemonade*, in 2016. All 12 songs made the *Billboard* Hot 100 chart at the same time.

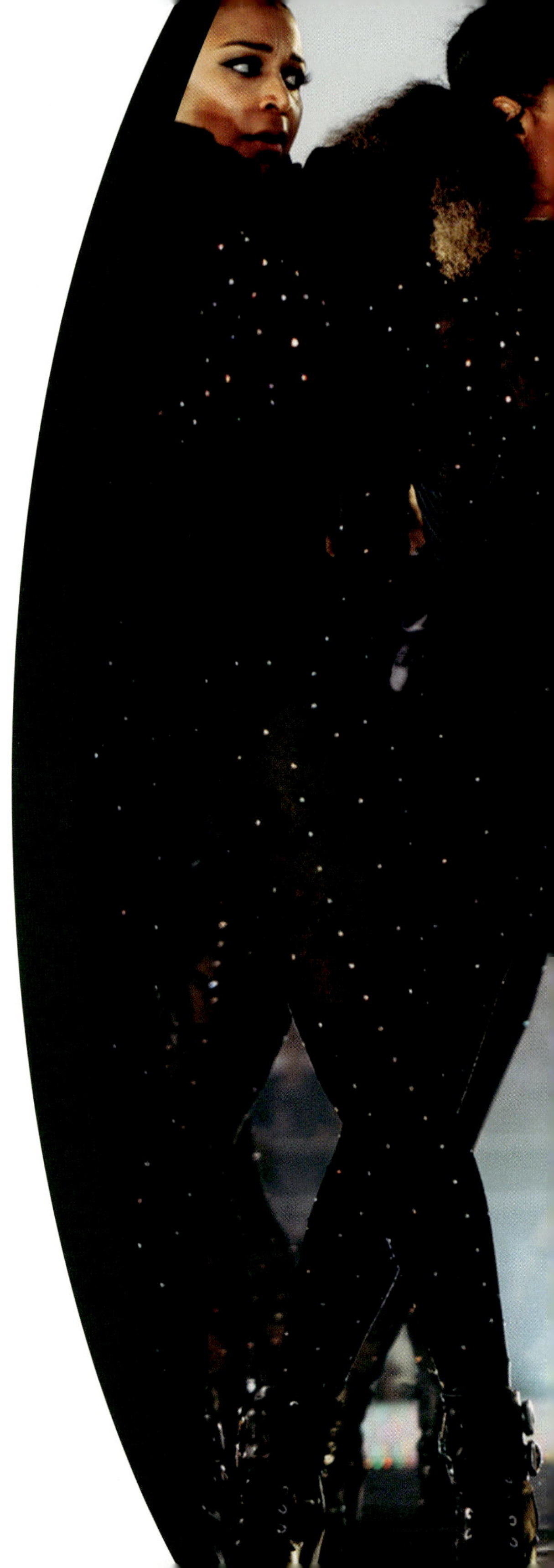

Beyoncé **debuted** her album *Renaissance* in 2022. She began her Renaissance World Tour in 2023. The tour broke ticket sales records worldwide!

Greatest of All Time

Beyoncé has been named one of the greatest vocalists of all time. Beyond music, she is a successful businesswoman, actress, and **director**. Beyoncé will continue to inspire people for years to come.

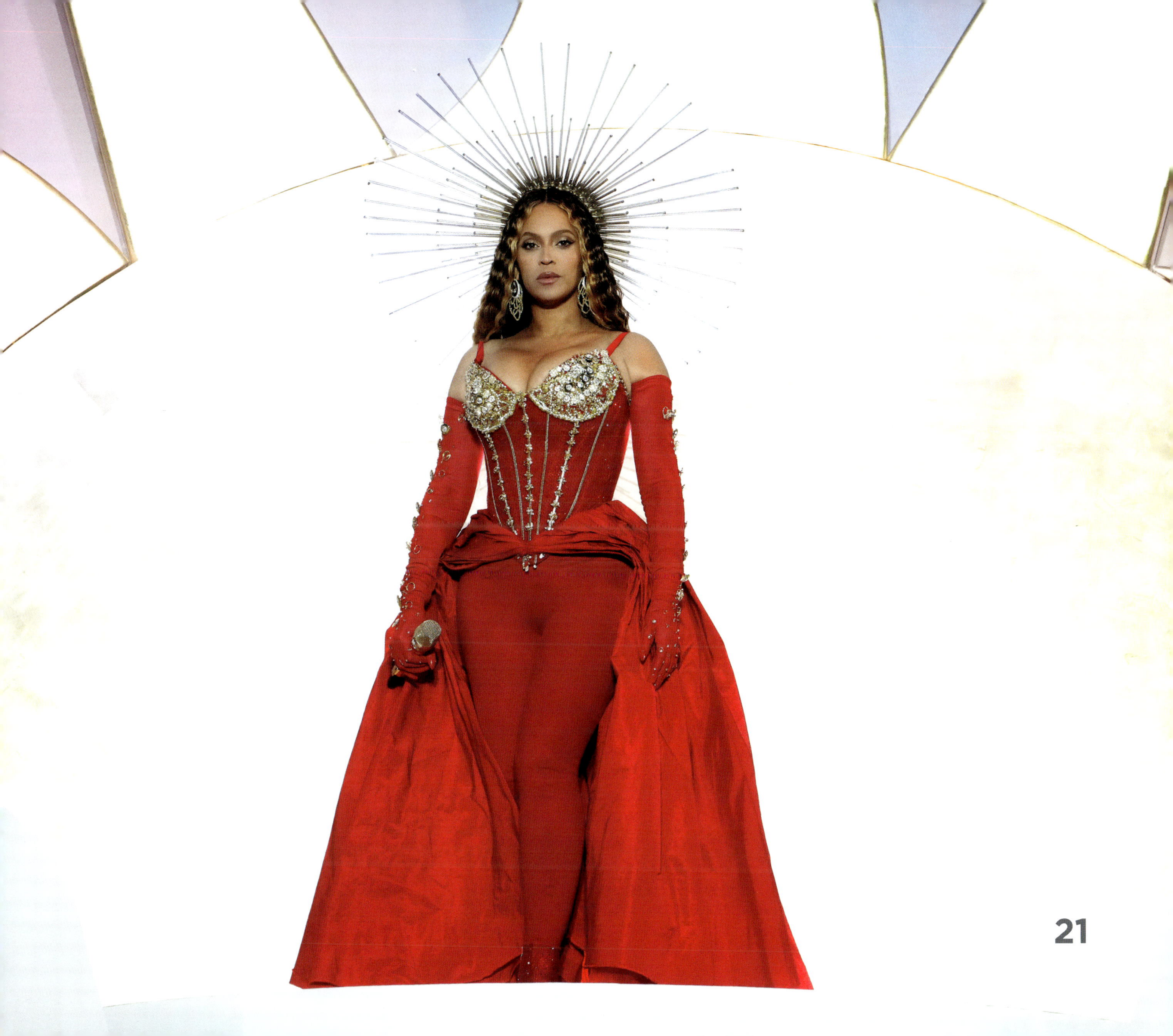

Career Highlights

1997 — Destiny's Child signs with Columbia Records. It becomes the biggest-selling female group of all time.

2001 — Beyoncé stars in her first film.

2003 — Beyoncé's first solo studio album, *Dangerously in Love*, is extremely successful.

January 2010 — Beyoncé breaks the record for most Grammy Awards won by a female artist in a single year.

2010 — Beyoncé decides to **manage** herself and launches her company Parkwood Entertainment.

2013 — Beyoncé directs her first movie *Life Is But a Dream*. She also performs at the Super Bowl halftime show.

2020 — *Black Is King*, a musical film, is released. It is codirected, cowritten, and starred in by Beyoncé.

2023 — Beyoncé makes history by earning the most Grammy Awards of all time.

Glossary

debut – to present to the public for the first time.

director – a person who guides actors and directs the performance of the script for a play or movie.

honor – a privilege that makes you feel proud.

inauguration – the ceremony of the person elected president officially becoming president.

manage – in the music industry, to oversee music production, performances, and promotion of an artist.

Index